stories from **India**

under the banyan

Eyes on the Peacock's Tail *a folktale from Rajasthan*
Magic Vessels *a folktale from Tamilnadu*
Hiss, Don't Bite! *a folktale from Bengal*
A Curly Tale *a folktale from Bihar*
All Free *a folktale from Gujarat*
Mazzoo Mazzoo *a folktale from Kashmir*
Wrestling Mania *a folktale from Punjab*
Sweet and Salty *a folktale from Andhra Pradesh*

Magic Vessels (English)
ISBN 81-86895-06-X

© Vayu Naidu (text)
© Tulika Publishers (illustrations)
First published in India, 1997
Reprinted 1998, 1999; this reprint 2003

Published by
Tulika Publishers, 13 Prithvi Avenue, Abhiramapuram, Chennai 600 018, India
email: kaka@tulikabooks.com OR tulikabooks@vsnl.com
website www.tulikabooks.com

Distributed by
Goodbooks Marketing Pvt. Ltd., 76 Fourth Street, Abhiramapuram, Chennai 600 018, India
email goodbuks@vsnl.com *website* www.goodbooksindia.com

Printed and bound at
indcom press, 393 Velachery Main Road, Vijaynagar, Velachery, Chennai 600042, India

For more information about Tulika or to order books visit our website.

www.tulikabooks.com

a folktale from tamilnadu

Magic Vessels

Tulika

by Vayu Naidu

art by Mugdha Shah

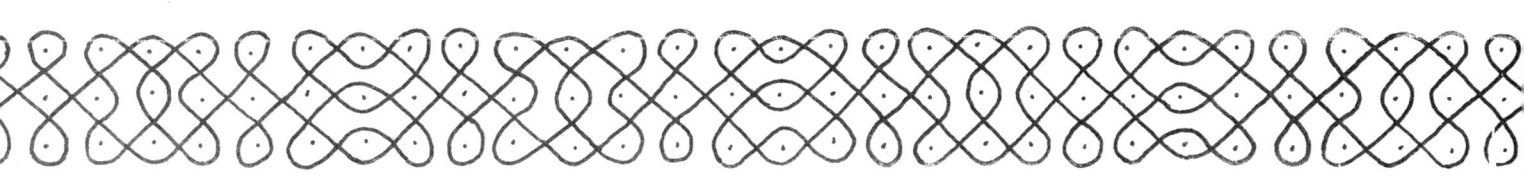

Muthu and Chellam lived in a banyan tree with eleven children. Muthu was a playwright. He wrote many plays. The people in the village loved his plays. But every time he made a little money, someone always borrowed it from him.

Chellam worked hard too. She cooked and cleaned in people's homes to put together a meal of sorts for her little ones. She also worried about the future. "Muthu," she said, "our Banyan is okay so long as the children are small. But what will we do when they grow taller?"

"Why do we need a house, Chellam?" he replied. "After all, Banyan has looked after us so well, so long. It will always take care of us. Stop worrying!" And he went back to writing.

However, Chellam continued to worry. So, one day, after the sun rose and the cock crowed, Chellam put some old cooked rice into a small pot, tied it with cloth, and gave it to her husband.

"Here, take this," she said. "Promise me you will try and earn some money this time."

"Okay!" Muthu replied. "I'll do my best." After all, Chellam worked so hard to take care of all of them.

So, off Muthu went through the forest. "How beautiful!" he said to himself as he saw the orange butterflies settling like flames on the creepers. Bees hummed. "Hey! I can catch the sun!" he laughed as he cupped his hands to hold the sunlight dancing between the leaves. Koels called in the distance.

Suddenly he came to a grove, and try as he might going this way and that, he always ended up in the same spot from where he started. The trees all seemed alike and every path looked like another. "I'm lost!" Muthu exclaimed, as he hung his pot on a branch. "And I feel so-o-o sleepy." The stream rippled a haunting tune and before he could rest his head comfortably on a pillow of leaves, he was fast asleep.

Now, in this forest lived little tree spirits. When they saw Muthu, they floated down from the branches, giggling and chattering. "Look!" said one, pointing at the pot. Eagerly they took down the pot and undid the cloth in which it was tied. A stale, sour smell wafted to their noses.

The tree spirits knew all about idli, masala dosa, sambar and mysore pak. But this green frothy thing was new. "Ummmm!" they chorused with great delight. In no time at all they licked the pot clean.

Muthu awoke. He was hungry, but the pot was empty! "Oh! What shall I do now?" he cried. Suddenly, near his foot, he saw a shining golden thing. "What's this?" he said and pulled it out of the earth. It was a small brass vessel. "If only I could have at least this much to eat!"

Immediately, down from the trees came the spirits. They spread a plantain leaf in front of Muthu. One spirit served him pickle, another chutney, then steaming rice and ghee. Golden-brown sambar was poured on the rice. It smelled so good. "Eat, friend!" the tree spirits said. Muthu ate and ate.

"That was great!" he said, licking his fingers when he finished. But when he looked up, the tree spirits had disappeared.

Muthu looked down at the vessel. "That's for you," soft voices said from the trees. "It's a magic vessel."

"Oh! Thank you, beautiful creatures of the forest!" Muthu said and hurried home.

It was evening. He could hear his hungry children crying. Muthu put the vessel down in front of his door. He lit a lamp, folded his hands and said: "I wish my wife and children could sleep on full stomachs tonight!"

From the branches of Banyan the tree spirits came down. They scrubbed the children clean. They oiled their hair and made them wear crisp new clothes. Then they fed them. The children ate so much and so well, they fell fast asleep right where they were sitting.

The next day, Muthu and Chellam threw a feast for everyone who had given them food when they had had none.

"We're going to eat in a poor man's house. Better eat before going," the village folk said to each other.

But what a surprise! The tree spirits gave them a meal fit for the gods! Delicious rice preparations, lots of mouth-watering vegetables, a variety of chips and pickles and an array of colourful sweets in different shapes were served to the guests. When some of them tried to slip sweets into the folds of their saris and lungis, the tree spirits rapped them on their wrists. "Whatever you eat, you eat here," they said.

Muthu and Chellam were the talk of the village for days.

The richest man in the village was the silk merchant, Kuppuswamy. Muthu had done many plays in his house but never once did Kuppuswamy give Muthu and his friends either meal or money.

Kuppuswamy got terribly jealous when he heard of Muthu's good luck. He too wanted a magic vessel.

"I will take a huge pot of lemon rice for the jungle creatures. They will give me a huge vessel in return," he thought to himself as he set out on his buffalo cart.

He came to the grove and went round in circles. Just as Muthu had done earlier. "Ayyo! What is this? My head is spinning!" he said. Suddenly Kuppuswamy heard the music of the stream. "I'll pretend to sleep," he said, and lay down. He was soon snoring.

The tree spirits saw what was happening and nodded to each other knowingly. They looked at the mountain of lemon rice and chuckled naughtily.

When Kuppuswamy awoke, there in front of his eyes was a huge vessel, an uruli. "Ha!" he said, gloating to himself. "A big vessel for a rich man!" The uruli was very heavy and Kuppuswamy had a hard time lifting it. Somehow he managed to push it into the cart. The buffalo groaned as it dragged the silk merchant and his newly-won uruli home in the hot sun.

As soon as he reached home, Kuppuswamy despatched a drummer into the village with an announcement. "Come one! Come all!" the man said. "There is a feast in the silk house tomorrow. Be there, or miss the treat of a lifetime!"

The people said to one another: "In a poor man's house the food was so tasty. In a rich man's house it will be better. Mmmm! Better starve, so we can eat our fill there!"

The village folk wore their best clothes and gathered outside the silk merchant's house. They looked hungrily at the magic vessel displayed proudly outside. The rich man cleared his throat and declared: "I wish my guests have a meal they will never forget!"

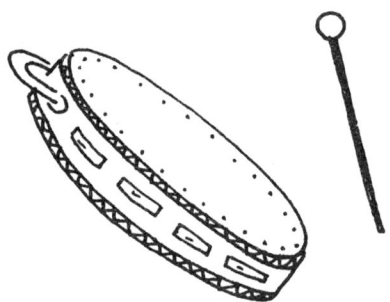

The wish had hardly left his mouth when swooosh! an army of roly-poly creatures bounced out of the vessel and began jumping at the guests. They had huge eyes and fierce moustaches. Grinning mischievously, they swung huge clubs. "Hu-ha!" they laughed. "You want a meal you will never forget? Here it is!" And they waved their clubs around wildly .

Screaming in shock, the people ran this way and that.

"Don't go! Don't go!" Kuppuswamy screamed after them. But who listened?

That evening, Muthu and his family gathered in a circle in front of old Banyan. Chellam lit a lamp and all the children bowed before it.

"Thank you, kind spirits," Chellam said. "Thank you for giving us this magic vessel. Now nobody will ever go hungry again."

The leaves of old Banyan rustled as a cool breeze blew. On that breeze floated a beautiful song. Muthu smiled at Chellam. "Our tree spirits are singing for us," he said. "Come, let us sing along." And they all joined in the singing.